How To Write

and Publish

A Cookbook

-

A Guide To Writing,
Self Publishing
and Selling A CookBook
With No Publisher Contract

without the fuss and stress of finding a publisher or agent,
without boxes of unsold books
lying around your home or garage,
even with no knowledge or understanding of advertising,
are not great with computers
and with ABSOLUTELY NO MONEY

Jen Carter

Table of Contents

"Keep away from people who try to
belittle your ambitions.

Small people always do that,
but the really great make you
feel that you, too,
can become great."

Mark Twain

Introduction

How to Write & Publish a Cookbook has been written to empower you to write and publish your own cookbook. Advances in technology and the popularity of the internet mean that it is now so easy to do. You really *can* do it. Even if you have been dreaming of writing it for years, now is the time to take advantage of the age of self-publishing and just go for it!

Modern printing technology means that you can hold in your hand a copy of your own cookbook, just a few days from approving the draft. Enjoy the achievement of being a published author, without breaking the bank.

We hold your hand and take you through the process of brainstorming what your book will be about, collecting and writing the recipes, putting the cookbook together, self-publishing and finishing with the joy of holding your very own recipe book in your hands with glowing pride and happiness.

So, what is my story and why am I qualified to write about this?

In early 2011 my daughter, Alissa, booked her flight to Australia where she was planning to live for six months. She was then faced with a period of three months before she could travel and wanted to use the time productively. After much thinking, we came up with the rather crazy idea that she should write her own cookbook. The idea of squeezing it into the short time available seemed challenging but attractive. We had been talking about it for so long, it was finally time to do it.

What we discovered was revolutionary! We learnt that you could publish and print your own cookbook for just a few dollars. We found that you didn't have to invest thousands of dollars to publish hundreds of books, to become a cookbook author.

We even found that you could publish your own ebook on big platforms such as the Amazon Kindle for no (or very little money), opening up your cookbook to a massive audience looking for instant online solutions.

Driven by this exciting revelation we realized that *anybody* with enough passion and drive could write and publish their own cook book on a really low budget. Using the latest technologies it is now possible to print each book on demand for incredibly low prices, currently (as at December 2011) less than $5 for a 100 page book.

Our own process was pressurised, going from starting the project, creating new recipes, testing existing recipes, to a draft manuscript in under three months. It took a further three months of editing and adjustments (mostly due to Alissa being in Australia, or it would have been shorter) before we were able to proudly publish her book and announce to our friends, family and the world that she was a published cookbook author.

If we had already had a cookbook ready to publish, the entire process could have taken less than a week. Simply incredible!

Since then, we have written and published a further three books using the same system and Alissa is currently working on her next book.

Getting Started

Writing a cookbook is easier than you think. You may have been conditioned to think that writing is for the experts, but an expert is only someone with a passion. Maybe someone *just like you*.

If you have ever dreamed of writing your own book, then writing a *cookbook* is a great idea. After all, everyone eats and most people enjoy food! What better genre to write for than one that's hungry (quite literally) for new and interesting ideas?

If you love to cook and share your recipes with friends and family, putting them in book form makes it even easier to share them with a wider audience, and a cookbook is one of the easiest books to write.

Cookbooks are always popular, they are one of the top best-selling book categories. People love reading cookbooks & trying out new recipes, cooks love to read them, give them as gifts or simply use them for inspiration.

You do not need formal training as a chef to publish your own cookbook. You do not even need to be a celebrity, so do not allow that to intimidate you. What you *will* require is a combination of patience and passion. Patience as you test recipes, rework, test again and make endless notes. Passion to help you carry through to the end, to share your recipes and to get your message across.

Why Write Your Own Cookbook?

Self publishing makes it possible for anyone who has a passion for food to write and publish their own cookbook.

Even just a few years ago if you chose to self-publish, you would often end up with hundreds of books stored in your garage and a massive printing bill for thousands of dollars. Today it is possible to economically publish books, publishing one at a time, for just a few dollars. You do not even need to carry any books in stock if you do not choose to.

Self publishing has been made so easy and affordable that the only question you need ask is "Is this something I would like to do?"

Julia Child wrote in order to share her passion for real French cooking with the American nation.

Julie Powell wrote her food blog about cooking as a challenge which later turned into a book and major movie deal.

Why do *you* want to write? What is your motivation?

Here's a few reasons that motivate people to achieve their goal of publishing their own cookbook:-

Share & spread a message or passion
Sharing your recipes or cooking style can be a major motivation.
Are friends always asking for copies of your recipes or saying that you should compile your own cookbook? Would you like to record your family recipes for your children or share them with friends? Would you like people to be inspired by a new style of cooking or share your passion about a particular ingredient?
Putting your recipes into a cookbook is a great way to share what you love.

Become A Published Author
You may always have dreamed of becoming an author one day. Writing your own cookbook could be your opportunity to become a published author. It can look great on your resume and impress potential employers.

Your friends and family may look on in awe and amazement as you show them your finished book. If sales go well you could become an *Amazon* bestselling author, or even a *New York Times* bestselling author, imagine the doors that might open up to you!

Create Publicity

If you have a cooking-related business, such as a restaurant, catering business or shop, a cookbook could help spread the word about you and attract new customers. It can even help build a following for you as a personality, your cookbooks, Twitter or YouTube channels or blog, all of which can lead you in other directions with your business. Consider the Hummingbird Bakery ... which came first, the bakery or the cookbook?

Earn Extra Money

Whether it is to earn some extra income or for fundraising, a cookbook has the potential to earn money. If you self-publish, you often get to keep more of the profit than if you work with a publisher. There is the potential to make more money if your book becomes popular. While few cookbook authors earn exceptional money, some earn enough to keep themselves comfortable.

Ebook sales have taken off explosively with the creation of e-readers such as the Kindle and Nook, ebooks have started to outsell print books.

By publishing your book as a paper book and also as an eBook, your book is available to a massive world market via Amazon. Your books could keep on earning you a small income for years with the right publicity, title and good reviews.

A Sense of Achievement
There is nothing quite like the joy and sense of achievement of holding a book you have written in your hands. It is an incredible moment when all that hard work comes together and your proof copy arrives.

Whatever your reason for writing a cookbook, it needs to be strong and powerful enough to help motivate you forward until you accomplish your goal!

What You'll Need To Get Started

Start with an old fashioned notebook or paper and pen or pencil. Keep your notebook in the kitchen and write detailed and legible notes as you create and work on recipes.

Equipment & Software

You will need to have access to a computer or laptop with a word processing program. If you're using a PC or laptop, you'll need software such as Open Office (free to download) or Microsoft Word. If you're on a Mac, you will need Open Office (free to download) or Pages.

For research and ideas, it would be good if you can have regular access to the internet, via a computer or smartphone. Reading blogs can really help to inspire and keep you from feeling you are on your own. Subscribe to a few of your favorite blogs can help you continue to feel inspired and encouraged, as well as part of a community of food-lovers.

Why not subscribe to a few to keep you feeling inspired and encouraged?

Your Minimum Budget

Although it is possible to create your first ebook with absolutely no money.

If you want to self publish your book, a minimum budget of $50-100 can help get you better results. You could spend far more depending on how professional you want it to look and how much help you will need along the way. However, the focus of this book is how to manage the process without breaking the bank!

The Where and Why Of Self Publishing

Why Self Publish?

Self publishing gives you complete control of your book, from content, look & feel to timetable. It puts you in the driving seat, setting you free from the need to find a publisher who likes your book enough to publish it.

Self publishing means that you can get your book published fast. If you're ready to publish, then you could hold your proof copy in your hands in as little as a week. With traditional publishers taking years to go through the complete process of publishing, taking matters into your own hands can cut that time down to months or even weeks.

Not only that, but you can be saved months or years of effort and heartache as you submit your book proposal to publishers only to receive rejections.

If you have heard or been told that self-publishing does not work, think again. "Rich Dad, Poor Dad" was originally self-published in 1997 and went on to become a bestseller, selling over 2 million copies. Self publishing might once have meant cheap and cheerful, but that is no longer the case.

Below I have sketched out a table of the time taken for three methods, traditional publishing, kindle publishing and self-publishing:-

TABLE	Traditional	Kindle	Self Publishing
Timescale	1-2 years	7-14 days	3-6 months
Finding an Agent	1-10 years	-	-
Cover	6-18 months	1 day	1-4 weeks
Start-Finished Book	18-36 months	1-7 days	1-8 weeks

With self publishing you have complete control over the timetable and it should take far less time until you actually hold the first proof copy of your book. These are two compelling reasons to choose the self-publishing route for your cookbook.

Benefits and Drawbacks of a Traditional Publisher

If you are intimidated by the process of self-publishing, you have two options. Slowly work through the process until you hold your book in your hands or find a publisher.

If you can find a publisher, realise that they do the editing, layout, publishing and distribution for your book. They may also give you an advance as you are writing the book. However, you will receive a lower income per book.

You would also have to be prepared to wait until a publisher accepts your book proposal, possibly submitting to dozens of publishers and going through the demoralizing process of receiving rejection letters until you are successful. Realistically, unless you have an agent, few publishers will even consider publishing your book.

Finding Your Great Idea

Once you have decided to write - it is time to get started, why wait one more day?

In your head and heart, there is a cookbook that only *you* can write. You have a unique mind and voice, so use them. Don't try and copy others, but write something that authentically reflects you and your unique interests and personality.

Whilst there are many ways of finding what to write about - the one essential ingredient for your book is that you must find something which you are *passionate* about. Writing a cookbook is hard work and takes commitment, you will need passion and enthusiasm to help carry you through.

It may be that you have a special interest that you have been wanting to write about for ages. For example, you are a vegan who needs a gluten free diet, you may already have some clear thoughts about what your cookbook will contain.

Your cookbook must also solve a problem, fill a need or help people in some way. For example, a cookbook on easy dairy free snacks for kids might be helpful and of interest to parents who discover their children are intolerant to dairy.

Cookbooks tend to fall into certain categories, you will probably find that you are drawn to creating a certain style of cookbook. Categories include ethnic and regional cooking, foods & ingredients, courses or dishes, diet-related, seasonal, health-based, fun (e.g. Roald Dahl's cookbook for kids), family recipes, cooking methods (e.g. baking, grilling), just to name a few to get you started!

What problem or interest will your book solve or appeal to?

Get Inspired - Seven Places To Find Great Ideas

If you really are stuck for what to write your cookbook about, it is time to get inspired. Here's seven places that can help get your brain popping with ideas:-

Pop into your local store which offers a wide selection of magazines - browse through them to spark ideas. Look at the adverts too, not just the articles. See what jumps out at your, captures your imagination or looks interesting.

Browse the Amazon book store - the books section will be divided up into section. Navigate to the 'Food & Drink' or 'Cooking, Food and Wine' section. As you click on each category, notice how it is broken down into smaller categories. You can even sort your searches to see what the bestselling books are in each category to see what's most popular at present.

Visit the library or used book store - see how they break down books into categories. Notice anything missing from their selection? Even the older more dated books could be inspiring, as you could bring your own special touch by updating them. Perhaps you could put a new spin on a classic style of cooking that reflects the latest in food fashions or techniques.

Personal interests - do you have personal interests related to food or health? For example, are you a mother with children at home, trying to cook healthy recipes for them? Check out the popular forums for those interests and see what questions people are asking or difficulties they are facing. Is there a cookbook which would help answer their questions or solve their problems?

Read blogs & websites - keep up-to-date with what others are doing. Food follows trends too. Are you good at looking ahead and spotting trends?

If you have an idea of what's about to trend and become popular, you can write your book as it grows in popularity. This gives you the potential to do well with sales of your book as well as having fun experimenting with new ingredients, food styles or techniques.

For example, cupcakes became incredibly popular in 2010, with everything featuring cupcake images or recipes. However, the trend had been building since 2007, with more and more people jumping on the cupcake bandwagon. Is there another trend that you can see ahead?

What is in the news? Are particular health issues hitting the headlines or has new research showed that a particular food has great benefits? Is there any way that you can use this to your advantage to help create something unique?

Discover what people are looking for - Google offer a great research tool to see what people are looking for. The Google Adwords keyword tool can help you if you've got a broad idea of what you're looking for, but want to drill down a little into specifics. It can help you find related ideas and brainstorm.

For example, you want to write about grilling, but do not know what people are searching for, you can use the tool to find out more. You might discover that lots of people are looking for "easy grilling recipes", could this help give you the detailed focus or even the title of your book?

This technique can also help when you are consider chapter titles and looking for ideas.

Talk with people - friends and family will know what you're most passionate about, what you love to talk about or cook. Ask them to suggest ideas of what your cookbook should be about.

Write down or record every idea that you have that excites and energises you and keep it safe and secure.

Writing What You Know
It may seem obvious, but writing what you know and following your passion can help create a great and inspiring cookbook.

Look at your own experiences and heritage. What is your family history, have you had any special training or experience with foods. For example, Tessa Kiros used her own unique heritage to create authentic and unique cookbooks (e.g. Falling Cloudberries, Tessa Kiros) that are treasured in kitchens across the country.

Explore your own special interests. For example, are you the person friends go to when they want an infallible cake recipe? Do you have a special love of using unusual ingredients? Have you adapted popular recipes to accommodate specific dietary requirements?

Look at your own recipe notes - do the recipes that you have created or refined have something in common that could become a cookbook some day?

If you are drawn to a popular subject, could you put your own spin on it? For example, writing about Indian cooking from the point of view of a novice.

Are there dozens of books on the subject you want to write about? If you can find a way to put a different twist on it, it means there is already a demand, and you can make work for you. Work on your ideas, refine them and write down your proposal.

Testing and Finalising Your Idea

After you have a list of all the ideas that came to mind as you researched and brainstormed, choose up to three ideas do you feel most excited and energised about.

Go through this simple checklist for each idea. Are you able to answer the following questions?

What problem will your book solve?
What kind of person will your book appeal to?
Is there demand for this kind of cookbook?
What makes your book unique and special?

As you are answering these, does one idea stand out as one that you have got the passion, experience *and* talent to write about? You will need all three to be able to craft a successful cookbook that you will be proud to publish.

If one idea stands out, write down a draft title for your book. Wait at least 24 hours.

How do you feel about this book idea - energetic & excited? If so, you have probably found your first cookbook to write. If not, go back through the process of finding and testing ideas again.

How do you feel now that you've chosen? Excited or anxious? If you are feeling anxious, go back and pick an idea that meets the criteria but that leaves you feeling optimistic and excited about what the future holds.

Do not worry that you may have to abandon some great ideas, you can always come back to them later when you have published your *first* cookbook!

Preparing and Writing Your Book

If, like most cooks, your cookbook notes resemble a pile of scrappy, barely legible notes, do not despair! It is possible to take these and create a great cookbook from such humble beginnings. It's just a matter of getting organised.

Who Are You Writing For?

Before you write a word, it can be helpful to consider just who you are writing for, what type of person is likely to buy it and just what makes it unique.

Build up a mental picture of the person you are writing your cookbook for. What are they like, what do they enjoy, how skilled a cook are they?

Consider where they might live, do they have a family, how do they spend their spare time? Most of all what is their special interest - for example, are they trying to slim, manage a gluten-free diet, or create a romantic meal.

If you have an idea of the type of person in your mind as you put together your recipes, it can help your book to have the right feel and be focused, rather than just a jumble of ideas. Before you start writing out any recipes, take a few minutes out to write a sentence or two explaining who you are writing for and what you want your book to achieve for your readers.

Finding Time & Being Disciplined

One question you must answer honestly before undertaking a cookbook is whether you have enough time. Will you be able to set aside time each week to cook and write. It doesn't matter if you can only find three twenty minute sessions each week, but you need to plan it in.

Without planning, it's too easy to procrastinate and never get around to even starting. It is likely that the entire project is going to take hours to write, so the best thing you can do is make a time and a date to start writing.

Initially you might find it quite hard to have the discipline to write your recipes down. Keep practicing, keep writing and taking notes and gradually your cookbook will come together. Nobody ever started out as an expert, they all got there through practice and persistence as well as a fair amount of hard work.

It may come as a surprise to you, but some of the most successful fiction writers have to shut themselves away and make themselves write. It doesn't somehow flow easily every day, they exercise self-discipline and make themselves write.

If you are goal-oriented, you may find it helpful to set weekly, daily or monthly targets - for example, 2 recipes created and written down each week or 1000 words written each month. Set small goals that help move you closer to your bigger goal of publishing your cookbook.

What Is Unique about Your Book?

With so many cookbooks already available, you need to consider what is special about the one you are going to write.

So, what is *your* hook? What is it that will make people buy your book? For example, "Easy to follow, sure-fire, cake recipes that can be enjoyed by diabetics".

This could be the unique spin that you put on it, your own experiences and background or personal interests.

Do you have a unique style of writing or a personality that comes across in the book?

Before You Get Started - Writing Your One Page Summary or Proposal

Write a one page summary of who the book is for, why you are writing it and what your readers will get out of it.

As you begin to write the book, this one page summary can help remind you of the purpose of the book. Though it's tempting to skip this step, this can really help in clarifying what you want to achieve and make the rest of the writing process more straight forward.

Come up with a "working" title and sub-title for the book, though you will probably change it before publication.

This is also a useful place to create draft chapter headings, that can help give you ideas for the types of recipes you need to research and create.

The process of working on this one-page summary can very helpful in clarifying what you want to achieve and can save hours of your time by giving you a clear aim and goal.

What Should I Include in My Book ?

Cookbooks tend to be rather more individual than other non-fiction books. Your book is as individual as you are. Here's some ideas of what you may wish to include in your book.

Beginnings

Your book should begin with a Title page, followed by a Copyright statement, Disclaimer and a Table of Contents. Your Copyright statement should include Copyright or © (year) by "your name".

Other things to include here could be an "About This Book", "Dedication", "Acknowledgements" or "Fore-word".

Recipes

How many recipes should you include in a cookbook? It is hard to say as it really is down to personal preference, but a minimum of 50-60 recipes would offer good value.

Your cookbook should probably be a minimum of around 80 pages, though it could be far more.

Of course, there are always exclusions to every 'rule', and if you feel you can offer just a collection of, say, 10 recipes in the Kindle format and people will pay for it, feel free to test it out.

Endings

The most important item to include at the end of your book is an Index. A good index is the key to finding recipes in any cookbook. If you do this yourself, it can be time-consuming, but is invaluable for your readers. You can also outsource this task to professionals who index cookbooks for a living. (See Appendix 2)

Your may also decide that your book should end with a Conclusion, About The Author, Resources and Appendices sections, it's up to your personal preference.

Putting Your Cookbook Together

There's rather more to putting together a cookbook than many people imagine. It is not just a case of writing down a few recipes, you'll need to spend time creating and testing recipes, writing them down, trying new ingredients, and finally you'll need to organise all these in an accessible way for publication.

Collecting, Creating & Testing Recipes

Most writers start by putting together all their notes and scraps of paper, to see what recipes they already have that they'd like to include in this cookbook. Making a list of these can help you identify what recipes you have already got, and help inform what recipes you are going to need to create or develop.

It is usual to use *original* recipes in your cookbook. There is some discussion as to what constitutes *"original"*, but most people agree that you need to change 2-5 things in any recipe to make it 'yours'.

If you are basing your recipe on another recipe, here are two important tips to follow. First, credit the original creator, second, write out the instructions and recipe in your own words. Whilst the list of ingredients is not copyrighted, the method or instructions is subject to copyright law.

You need to ensure that each recipe in your cookbook has been tested. The easiest way to test is to make sure that you have cooked the final version of each recipe yourself.

Why not can make testing fun, invite friends and family round to taste your new dishes. You may need to cook some recipes several times to find out the best ingredients, measurements, times and temperatures for each dish.

Recipe Writing Tips
Whenever you are testing a new recipe, it's essential that you record everything. You need to record a detailed list of each ingredient and the quantity used. Record how many servings your recipe will make, time and temperature of cooking, etc.
Decide how you are going to record your measurements, either in metric (grams), cups or imperial (ounces).

Create a list of standard abbreviations and capitalizations for common terms. For example, are you going to write "teaspoons" or "tsps", "Tbsp" or "tbsp". Whatever you choose, you need to write it the same way in every recipe in the book.

To prepare your recipe for publication, list each ingredient in the order you use them. Write out step by step, easy to understand instructions.

Check each recipe by ensuring that all the ingredients in the ingredients list are actually included in your recipe - it is surprisingly easy to overlook this basic check. Check that each recipe includes how many servings it will make, cooking temperature and cooking time.

Now that you have collected all the recipes for your book, one of the biggest challenges is how you're going to organize them and layout the book.

Organising Chapters

It is helpful for your readers if you can somehow, break down all your recipes into chapters.

Have a look at your favorite cookbooks - how are they organized? How you organize your book is your decision, popular ways include organizing by type of meal or ingredient.

Write a list of the recipes that you are hoping to include in the book. Do some of them have common elements, similarities or would they just naturally group together? When organizing recipes into chapters, consider that this helps your reader to see, at a glance, what they are likely to find in your cookbook. So make it sound tempting.

For example, in Alissa's *"Healthy Breakfast Recipes"* book, she organised the recipes under the following chapter headings:-

Traditional Breakfasts
Breads, Loaves & Rolls
Fruit & Berries
Pancakes & Waffles
Smoothies, Shakes & Drinks
Brunch & Special Occasions
Around The World & European
Eggs, Scrambles & Omelettes
Spreads, Butters and Jams
On The Go

As you can see, the way that you organize your recipes can be as unique as you wish or relevant to your own subject area.

Creating A Professional Layout

After you have decided on how you are going to organize your recipes with chapter headings, you may want to consider how the cookbook itself is laid out.

It's important that the interior of your book is easy to read, and that the recipes are well laid out and easy to follow.

You will need to consider information such as:-

book size & format - do you want a paperback, hardback or are you happy with just Kindle? It can help to revisit your motivation for wanting to write a cookbook at this point - you can get your ideas out there with a Kindle, but if you really want to hold your cookbook in your hands, then your choice is easy, choose Createspace.

budget - what sort of money do you want to spend on editing, design, publishing & promotion? If you're on a low budget or no-budget, start with Kindle and see whether your book sells. Once you can see it selling and increasing in popularity on Kindle, you may then want to consider making it available as a traditional book by printing and publishing through Createspace.

white space - you need white space around the page so that it doesn't feel crowded. Do not feel that you have to fill every space with text, be aware of margins, line and letter spacings too.

page numbers - if you are publishing a paperbook, rather than an ebook, you will probably want to include page numbers. Do you want these at the bottom of the page, the top, the centre, the corner. Have a look at books that you enjoy using most and decide which you prefer.

fonts - possibly one of the most important decisions you'll make in terms of the appearance of your book. Fonts to consider include Georgia, Verdana, American Type, Garamond or Palatino. Do not be tempted to use Times New Roman or whatever you normally use on your computer, as this font does not look right in book format.

Using Photos, Illustrations and Drawings
Most of the cookbooks on your bookshelf may include photos, so it's reasonable to assume that you would be

expected to include images in your own book. Yet this assumption is gradually being eroded with the trend towards digital books, such as Kindle.

It is clear that people are happy to buy cookbooks *without* images. Indeed, some of the most popular paperback cookbooks do not have any photographs, except for on the cover. Many people are now looking for convenience, they want their recipes at their fingertips, on their PC, Mac, iPad or smartphone.

Any photos you do use need to be top quality as people are used to seeing great photos in magazines and online. If you choose to use photos, these images are what most people will be buying the book for, so make sure they're professional and laid out beautifully. Quality is not just about a high resolution image. It is about an image that is well-styled and attractive to the eye.

Unless you are a very experienced photographer or blogger, you are unlikely to be able to setup photos that are of sufficient quality. Some self-published books have included photos which are taken by the author, however they can give the book an "amateur" feel, especially when used on the cover.

To sell your book it needs to have a professional look and feel. If you need to hire a photographer and/or food stylist, this is going to add hundreds, if not thousands of dollars to your book budget. Therefore, if you can, for your first cookbook, try to work in black and white, and without photos.

Once you have gained experience of the writing and publishing process, then you may wish to consider moving on to your 'dream' book which includes dozens of beautifully styled colour photographs. A larger budget can allow you to invest in professionals to make your book beautifully illustrated and tempting to the eye.

Here's some bestselling cookbooks that have become successful without including photographs:-

"Real Fast Food" (Nigel Slater)
"Fast Cakes" (Mary Berry)
"How to feed your whole family a healthy, balanced diet" (Gill Holcombe)

If you are still keen to include some images in your book, consider adding some line drawings to illustrate the book. This is what bestselling cookbook author Julia Child did with her masterpiece, "Mastering the Art of

French Cooking" which includes drawings and illustrations (based on photographs) from her husband Paul and Sidonie Coryn. If you are on a budget, but keen to include images, using illustrations could be an avenue to explore. Always ensure that you have the right to use any images you use!

In Alissa's "Healthy Breakfast Recipes" book, she wanted to include some imagery but her budget for the entire project was around $100. She succeeded in finding someone who would do simple line drawings, to include with each chapter heading, giving the book character.

Crafting the Right Title for your Book
Great titles sell books, it is that simple.

The truth is, your title can make or break for your book, so it is essential to spend time considering what the right title should be for your cookbook. The title should be clear, enticing and make the subject matter of the book clear, perhaps with a subtitle to draw the reader in.

Here's a few great titles that really work:-
Nosh for Students: A Fun Student Cookbook
Hamlyn All Colour Cookbook 200 Cupcakes

The 4-Hour Body: An uncommon guide to rapid fat-loss, incredible sex and becoming superhuman: The Secrets and Science of Rapid Body Transformation

The Curry Secret: How to Cook Real Indian Restaurant Meals at Home

Rosemary Conley's Amazing Inch Loss Plan: Lose a Stone in a Month

Slow Cooking Properly Explained: Over 100 Favourite Recipes

Baby-led Weaning: Helping Your Baby to Love Good Food

These titles are taken from a list of Amazon best-selling recipe books.

You will notice that they all have several things in common:-
- a clear title that explains what the book offers
- a sub-title then draws you in to discover more clear benefits that you will receive on buying the book (e.g. cook indian meals at home, help your baby love good food, transform your body).

The process of writing the perfect title can take days, weeks or months. The good news is that you do not have to decide on your title until your book is finished. However, it can be helpful to jot down several ideas for both your title and subtitle as you go through the writing process. So why not brainstorm some ideas for titles and write down a shortlist of the best that you come up with.

Once your cookbook is finished, you can return to these ideas to see more clearly which title and subtitle combination could really work. If the title choice is not clear to you, or there are several contenders, why not ask friends for help?

You may have favorites or ideas that you love that really aren't going to work in the marketplace. Your friends can help you weed these out and find what would appeal to potential readers.

Write or print a few combinations of title and subtitle on to paper. Ask your friends to be honet with you and either pick their favorites or grade them from most attention grabbing to least. (This process can also be a great way of helping select your book cover, if you end up with more than one choice)

Write down your final selection of title and subtitle combination - put this up on a wall or somewhere where you will see it daily. Let your subconscious do the work of seeing if there is any way that you can improve on this title. Keep improving it until you are 100% happy with your cookbook title.

Editing, Formatting & Layout - In-house or out-sourcing?

One of the hardest tasks, after testing all those recipes, is to create the draft document for your book. If you are publishing an ebook on Kindle, this is something you can do fairly easily yourself.

However, if you are planning to publish on Createspace, you will want your book to look good as well as offering great recipe ideas.

There are several options for you:-

Do It Yourself - Even if you have an eagle eye, you will almost certainly have missed some spelling mistakes or simple errors. Asking a friend or family member to go through your draft manuscript carefully can help you locate and correct these errors.

If you are fairly competent in your Word Processing program, you may be happy to take on the formatting and page layout yourself. If you follow this route, you may wish to base your layout on your own favorite cookbook, or another self-published book whose layout you like.

Outsource - you can find recommended individuals or companies to work on your book at www.Elance.com. You will find editors - it's probably best to ensure that these are native English speakers for the best results. For layout and formatting, you will find providers who are prepared to do this for as little as $50. Ensure that you check their portfolio to see if they are up to successfully completing the task.

Go Professional - there are many online businesses that specialise in formatting and layout, so that your cookbook looks professional. The costs can range from just a few dollars to hundreds or even thousands.

The Secret to Success - The All-Important Cover
Covers sell books. It's that simple. Big secret to success, right there!

There is no doubt about it - whether it is in a bookshop, with people picking up the books with attractive covers, or on Amazon where people click to find out more on books whose cover and title grabs their attention.

Your cover is not a place to skimp on funds if you want to produce a cookbook that attracts sales.

So, how do you great a great cover on a budget?

You will probably need a great image for your cookbook cover, though you may discover that text on a plain background is more popular for your type of book.

If you are selling on Amazon, your cover needs to look great as a small image, known as a 'thumbnail'. If you are publishing a paperback you will need to create a cover which includes front cover, spine and back cover.
The cookbook cover should reflect the contents, style and feel of the book itself. How you do that will depend on your own personal tastes.

If you are publishing solely on Amazon Kindle, you could just use an image without any text. As they say, "A picture is worth a thousand words".

For an example, check out "Great Greek Food: The Ultimate Collection Of The World's Finest Greek Food Recipes" in the Kindle store. It uses a lovely attractive image from the rooftops of Santorini and has been a best-selling cookbook. If you have a great photo that shows the best of what is in your cookbook, trim it to landscape format and use this as your cover.

If you need an image, but do not have a photograph, check out the suggested websites to find photos in the Resources section (Appendix 2) to buy a copyright-free image that you can use.

Do some research. Go to Amazon.com to see cookbooks, similar to yours, that are selling well. Navigate down through the categories to find books on food and cooking. Amazon allows you to sort by bestselling, so use this tool to see what the covers for the bestselling books look like.

If you are able, print out the first two pages of bestselling cookbook covers, to provide ideas and inspiration. Make a note of the covers which grab your attention and see what they have in common. Is there a common type of image, image/text combination, style or color that is used? This could help inform your choice of your own cover.

You can also find people who will create a great cover for you for upwards of $50 dollars on Elance.com or guru.com. If you are publishing first on Kindle, you can save this expense and get a cover created on Fiverr.com for just $5 .

Choose someone who's sample designs are similar to what you require, so that you know that they are capable of producing the kind of image that you desire. If you are working with a provider from Fiverr.com, you may need to buy the rights to the image for them to work with from one of the stock photo companies, in order to ensure you do not breach copyright law.

When you publish a paperback via Createspace, a professional cover is likely to bring in more sales than a home-created image. You can create your own free cover using the free tools at Picnik.com. You will need an image or background to start with, then crop image to size and add text for title, subtitle and backcover.

Proof reading

Once you have put everything together, recipes, chapters, ingredient lists, introduction and About The Author, set it aside for a week. This gives you time to be able to view what you have created more objectively.

Now print out your draft so that you can read through and spot obvious errors, typos and mistakes. Then check for accuracy for cooking times, ingredients, measurements, instructions, recipe by recipe, this can be a long task, requiring several breaks and plenty of hot drinks.

Make all your amendments on your draft copy, then up-date your master copy on the computer.

You are now ready to publish your book!

The Perfect Price

Once the process of drafting your book is complete, you are ready to upload and publish your book. However, there's one more key decision that you need to make, how much are you going to sell it for?

This may be determined by your own costs, your desire to sell as many as possible, or your desire to market it as an exclusive item. The choice is yours.

When determining the price to sell on Kindle, you have two royalty options. You can choose a price that allows you to set it at 70% royalty, or at 35% royalty. (See Appendix 1)

One popular option is to discount your final price for a few weeks as you launch your book as a special "deal" for friends, family and followers. This can help kick sales off to a good start, giving you a good ranking in Amazon and improving the visibility of the book.

The good news is that, whatever price you choose, it is simple to change it through Createspace or Kindle. Once sales have kicked off, you can test different prices to see how it affects your sales, to see what the right price for your cookbook is.

Where To Self Publish Your Book

Once you are ready to publish your book, you will probably start to notice all sorts of websites and publishers that promise to help you with the process. Most of them will charge you a considerable sum for their "help" and assistance. The truth is that you can do a credibly good job yourself.

There are two ways to publish that we have used and recommend, Createspace and Kindle, both of which are owned by Amazon.

These are not the only ways to self-publish, but they are very user friendly and interact with the Amazon online store which is one of the most popular online stores for books and ebooks.

Kindle is Amazon's ebook (digital book) publishing platform. The beauty of publishing your book to Kindle is the ease with which you can upload it, test out different titles and make your book available for instant delivery worldwide.

Createspace allows you to create your own print (paper) book. There is no setup cost, your only cost is the price for printing and posting your proof copy (approx $10-20). If you want to make your book widely available, it is simple to select this through the Createspace marketing options ("make your book available in book stores").

Kindle

With ebook sales growing phenomenally, the Kindle is a popular and profitable market that can get you earning money within hours of making your book live on Amazon. It is also a great way of testing the market for your book without the layout and cover requirements of a paper book.

Publishing with Kindle is a great first step for any would-be cookbook writer. It allows you to learn the process of putting together a cookbook without the pressure of having to come up with hundreds of recipes.

Simply putting together a collection of recipes that you have already tested means you can get a cookbook published quickly, learn and understand the process, preparing you for the process when you want to publish your "dream cookbook".

If you are offering something specialised - for example "gluten-free cupcakes", you can probably publish a cookbook with as few as 20 recipes. If you already have these recipes prepared, your cookbook could be available and published on Amazon Kindle in less than a week.

The Kindle platform also makes it easy to test how changes affect sales. For example, you can test how well different covers sell, the effect of price changes on sales, helps you work on crafting a good description. You will notice that adding a good subtitle, that includes keywords (words people type into the search engines, such as Google or Amazon), to your book can impact sales.

Publishing on Kindle requires no expertise, takes less input and effort, and is a good preparation for the launch of a paperback or hardback cookbook later on.

Createspace

This Amazon publisher makes it easy to publish your book, even if you are not technically minded. Using advanced technology, Createspace literally prints your books on demand, whenever one is ordered. It is now as easy and quick to print one copy of your book as it used to be to make a photocopy.

Publishing with Createspace can allow your book to be available in bookstores across the country, depending on what marketing options you choose and how much profit you wish to make.

Createspace allows you to set the price of your book and choose options which give you the best royalty options using the "Royalty Calculator". It's up to you to work and see how you balance price and sales, to find the perfect balance for each book.

How To Publish on Kindle

If you have an Amazon account, and a Word Processing program, you can publish on Kindle.

To take a look at Kindle publishing, go to http://kdp.amazon.com (log in here, irrespective of the country you are based in) and log in using your Amazon account. If you don't already have an Amazon account, you will need to create one.

There are several 'tabs' to browse through. "Bookshelf" shows all the book titles that you are working on or have already published. "Reports" shows sales of your books in all the countries where you book is available. "Community" is a forum which can help you solve common problems or communicate with other authors.

Once your book is ready for publishing, choose "Add new title" from the menu. You are then be prompted to enter some specific details for your book.

Book name:- this should be the punchy title and subtitle that you have created, which include the keywords that you researched earlier.

Description:- This is an opportunity to give potential readers a taster of what is in your book. You should aim to write at least 250+ words, which include some of the words or phrases that you know people looking for this type of recipe or cookbook might be looking for. These are words and phrases that you found when doing your keyword research.

It might be helpful to potential readers if you can give an idea of chapter headings or subjects covered. It is also appropriate to write something "About the Author" which gives something of your own background and reasons for writing the book. If you get stuck for words, click over to Amazon and get some inspiration by seeing what sorts of things others have written about.

Book contributors:- This is where you get to add your name as author or editor of the book. You will notice that you need to add your first name and surname. You also get to select your 'contribution', allowing your name to be displayed as either author, editor or illustrator, etc. It is possible to co-author with another individual and for you both get listed as authors.

Verifying Your Publishing Rights:- As this is your own work, sign up to say "This is not a public domain work".

Target Your Book To Customers:-

Choosing *categories* within Amazon may take some time, if you are new to the process. Start by navigating to the "Cooking" section and browsing the sub-categories within this for the most appropriate. If your book also is aimed at individuals with specific health issues (for example, diabetes), you may also wish to select the appropriate condition under "Health and Fitness".

Search keywords - you can choose up to seven keywords, separated by commas, that people are likely to search for. For example, for Alissa's breakfast cookbook, this could have been :- brunch,breakfast recipes,diabetic recipes,diabetes,healthy breakfast,romantic breakfast, bircher muesli Your own list should come from a combination of your earlier keyword research but also your own idea of the phrases most likely to be associated with your cookbook.

Upload Your Book Cover:- At this point, you should already have created or designed your cover art. There are a handful of requirements from Amazon that you will need to meet - these are currently (December 2011) that the image dimensions are at least 500 by 800 pixels, with a maximum of 2000 pixels on the longest side, saved at 72 dots per inch (dpi) for optimal viewing. If you are not sure whether your image meets these requirements, open it up in Picnik.com and see the dimensions under the "save and share" option.

To upload, navigate to the image on your computer and click open, then "upload image", now wait until you see that it has "uploaded successfully". Now you will be able to see a preview of your cover image. If you are not happy with it, you can amend and upload it multiple times until you are happy with the preview image.

Upload Your Book File:-
DRM - We suggest that you select "Enable digital rights management", which means Kindle files cannot be shared with other users. In addition, it means that the original file may not be downloaded and shared else-where. Digital Rights Management (DRM) is designed to inhibit unauthorized access to or copying of digital content files for your titles.

If you prefer to share your book, make sure that you are aware of the potential implications of sharing, as you cannot change this option at a later date.

Your book should be in html or .doc (NOT .docx) format, ready to upload. Click "Browse for book", navigate to the file on your computer and select the appropriate file. You are now ready to "Upload book", this process can take around a minute, depending on the size of your book. Once complete, you will be able to "Preview book" to see how it will look on a Kindle.

It's likely that you will need to make adjustments to the formatting, especially page breaks and carriage returns, to make sure that the final file that you upload looks great in the Preview. Keep working on the format and re-uploading until you are happy with how the Preview looks.

If you are struggling with this, one system that seems to work well is to upload a Word document to Open Office (a free program for both PC and Mac), then save as an html file. This can often help get rid of any strange formatting errors that you are encountering.

Continue to amend your original file, uploading and pre-viewing it until you are happy with how your book will look.

Done? Great, that is the hardest part completed!

Verifying Your Publishing Territories:- Since this is your own work, select "Worldwide rights - all territories".

Choose Your Royalty:- As discussed earlier, and in Appendix 1, the 70% royalty option is the most profitable choice for most authors. Pricing your book between the minimum and maximum list prices ($2.99-$9.99, £1.49-£6.99, 2.60-8.69 Euros, as at July 2012) allows you to receive 70% royalty from qualifying sales.

Initially, you will need to select your sales price in US Dollars. Your choice of price depends on how much value you place on your work, but also whether you want to encourage early sales. This is a tough balance to find, have a look to see what similar or comparable books are costing on Kindle can be most helpful in finding the right price for your potential market.

As well as the US there are a number of other markets open for you to sell in, you can either set these prices directly if you are familiar with the currencies or select the "set price automatically based on US price" option, which calculates these prices for you.

Kindle Book Lending:-

This option is not recommended for non-fiction writers whose readers are looking for a quick solution. For cookbook authors, I would suggest that you *do not* "Allow lending for this book" as there is no reason or inducement for borrowers to later buy your book for themselves.

Read the disclaimer and select the box to confirm that you have the rights to publish the book.

If you are still working on aspects of the book, such as Title, Description or Cover, you can select "Save For Later" at this point.

Once you are ready for the book to go live on Amazon, select "Save and Publish". This will then submit your book for the review process, which takes around 24-48 hours. During this time, you will not be able to edit any aspect of your book, and it will show on your Bookshelf as in "review".

Once approved, your book will show as "Live" and will appear on Amazon for purchases.

Congratulations, you are now a published author!

How To Publish on Createspace

In order to publish on Createspace you will first need to set up an account with them. You then have an opportunity to market your book, using the Title and Book Description to entice potential readers. Your cover is also an important marketing tool, so ensure that you have a strong cover image, as well as well written back cover copy, which includes your "About The Author" information.

For your cover, there are two options. You can use their Cover Creator design tool, make a Basic Cover based on the physical properties of your book (e.g. white or cream paper, number of pages) or have one designed to your specifications. Once you have finalised the cover, upload in Createspace.

Every printed book requires an ISBN (International Standard Book Number) to uniquely identify it. Createspace offers you the option to select a Createspace allocated ISBN number, saving on the trouble and cost of purchasing your own ISBN and they make no charge for providing it. It is possible to buy your own ISBN, but if you are only planning on publishing one book, it is probably not something you need to do. (See Appendix 2 for where to purchase ISBN's)

Createspace offer downloadable Word document templates for each book size they offer , currently over 15, allowing you to create the perfect layout for your interior. Once you have written and finalised your book interior, simply export it as a PDF and upload in Createspace.

When you are happy with both the interior and cover, you can complete the setup and submit your files for review. The Createspace review process takes 24-48 hours. During this time the interior and cover are checked to ensure that they meet the required standards. If they do not meet the standards, you will be sent a message advising you what the problem is so that you can correct and resubmit.

When the review process is complete, it is time to order a proof copy of your book. This allows you to approve the book and make it available for sale through Amazon and other channels. At the time of writing in 2011, it is possible to approve the book without seeing a proof copy, which we would *not* recommend for first-time publishers. However, this option may be helpful if you are simply making minor changes or updates to an existing book.

Amazon offers a range of shipping options, depending on your budget and sense of urgency. It is possible to hold a proof copy of your book in your hand a few days, possibly a week, after you place your proof copy order.

If you get the editing and cover right, your book can look just as high a quality as anything you see in your local bookshop.

Reviewing Your Createspace Proof Copy

There's few things that compare to holding a book that you have written and published for the first time. After the days and weeks of writing and preparation, it is an incredibly special moment to see your own work in print.

Once your proof copy arrives, it is time to check the details and correct any errors. Check your cover images, also spelling and text on the front and back of the cover. Check that any wording on the spine reads well and is clear. ·

For the interior, check that the layout is inviting and easy to read. Have you chosen the right font and spacing, or does it need tweaking? Check the look of your chapter headings and subheadings - are you happy with the font, is the font size right? Look at the page margins - are they too big with too much white space, or too small with the words seeming crowded on the page? Are any images or tables printed clearly and in the right place? If you have included page numbers, book title, chapter titles, do they work well or do they distract from the main text?

These are just a few of the questions you should ask yourself if you have created the interior layout yourself. As you can see, there are many issues to consider, which is why this is one of the areas where spending money on an expert can be a good investment.

If there are changes to be made, you will need to adjust your interior file, submit for review, and order a further proof copy until you are happy that your book is ready for sale to the public.

Once you are happy with the proof copy, it is time to approve your book on Createspace. Within 24 hours you should see it available for sale on Amazon, you are now a published author!

Promoting & Selling Your Cookbook

Now that your cookbook is successfully completed and published, you can focus more on promoting and selling your book.

This is one of the few times you are allowed to brag and promote yourself, so feel free to blow your own trumpet and let everyone know that you are now a cookbook author!

Just a few years ago, trying to sell copies of your book was incredibly hard and time-consuming work. Of course, you do not have to promote your book if you are just planning to sell it to family and friends.

The wonder of Amazon is that they will sell your cookbook for you and it will not cost you anything. Even if you publish through Amazon Kindle or Createspace, you will probably sell a handful of books. By selling through Amazon's book store you will be reaching a massive, worldwide audience of book lovers. If you wish to make your book available elsewhere, consider promoting on other platforms such as Smashwords and Barnes & Noble.

If you want to promote your book further, either to get know as an author or to start making money from your writing, then this is where the hard work really starts.

Many authors are surprised to find that there is just as much work involved in promoting your book as there is in actually writing it.

If you do want to promote, Appendix 2 includes some great resources.

However, here's some ideas that you might find useful to start you thinking about what will work for you and your book.

Amazon

Once your book is listed on Amazon there are several things you can do to promote it. Ask friends who have read your book to "tag", "like" or review your book. Potential buyers love to see honest reviews of books and this makes them more inclined to buy. If you have connections with people who could review your book, either send them a review copy or send them the PDF file of the book to review. Use the reviews in your publicity, on your blog, website or in your book itself.

KDP Select

This is a program available through Kindle to make your book available free for a limited time. This offers the possibility of gaining reviews, increasing your visibility and increasing sales of your books through Createspace. It also offers an additional revenue opportunity, as you receive payment for people borrowing your book on Amazon.com. This may not work for everyone, but is certainly worth experimenting with for your book.

Socialise

Are you part of an active network on social sites such as Twitter and Facebook. Use social networking to interact with your potential audience.

Be The Expert

Write articles, hang out in forums, send media releases, do guest blog posts, be interviewed, create a podcast - do whatever works for you to be perceived as an expert in your field.

Develop A Following

Use sites such as YouTube and your blog to develop a following. Promote subscribers via YouTube or get people to sign up via Feedburner to receive updates on your site. Create content - whether it's blog posts, videos or whatever - engage with your potential audience.

Create A Bestseller

An increasing number of writers are working to achieve "bestseller" status on Amazon. By becoming one of the top sellers in a category for a few hours, which will mean you can call yourself an "Amazon bestselling author". The basic idea behind the Bestseller Strategy is to promote your book in dozens of places on just one day, often by creating an irresistible special offer to encourage people to buy.

Brainstorm Ideas

Everyone is unique and has different strengths. Get a blank piece of paper and write down as many ideas for promoting your book as you can think of.

Consider your background, involvement and network and what ways you can use this to your advantage.

Self Publishing Success Stories

The publishing world is changing, fast. When John Locke, a self published author, sold over 1 million Kindle books it was a massive milestone. It showed that anyone with enough energy, interest and skill had a chance to make it big in the writing world.

Here's a few individuals who started by self-publishing and have gone on to become successful cookbook writers:-

Bruce Cadle (romantic meals)- blogger from Muy Bueno published "Party for Two" to promote husbands cooking for their wives on date nights.

Paula Deen (southern cooking) - started her cooking business after the breakup of her marriage. She went on to self-publish "The Lady & Sons Savannah Country Cooking" full of traditional Southern recipes. The book was noticed by a literary agent of a major publishing house and Paula has gone on to stardom on the Food Network as well as featuring in the movie Elizabethtown. Paula has gone on to write a number of popular books on Southern cooking.

Rose Elliot (vegetarian) - Rose published her first cookbook, "Simply Delicious", through her family publisher, The White Eagle Publishing Trust in 1967. She sent her book out to a number of magazines and newspapers , creating demand from bookshops and launching her career as a cookery writer. Her second book, "Not Just A Load of Old Lentils", self-published in 1972, was followed by publication of dozens of books on vegetarian cookery through traditional publishers.

Could the next self-published best-selling book have your name on the front cover?

What Do I Do Now?

How Much Could I Earn?

If you have followed some of the tips in this book, you are probably already ahead of the clueless writer that just makes their book available through Kindle or Createspace.

It is likely that you will find you sell a few books each month, and that your sales will build up over time.

You are likely to spend hours on your cookbook, so if you're looking at an hourly rate of pay, publishing a cookbook is not very well paid.

How much you earn will depend on how good you are at coming up with original recipes, the demand for the type of recipes you write and how many formats you offer your books in (e.g. Kindle, Createspace, Smashwords, etc).

If you really want to build a following, get yourself a blog or YouTube channel, get people to subscribe, and sell your books there too. If you sign up as an Amazon affiliate, you will also get a percentage of any Amazon sales from your blog or website.

To summarise, you are unlikely to get rich. You could, but do not count on it. Don't quit your day job yet!

Fundraising Cookbooks

Using Createspace to set up your charity fundraising cookbook is virtually risk-free. You have minimal set up costs and with the rise of social media such as Twitter and Facebook, it is easy to promote your book online to a wide audience.

Keep Going Until You Get Lucky

Your first book may not sell well, in fact it may sell only a handful of copies.

However, persistence is the key - keep putting your books out there. Learn about writing. Learn about promotion - this is the key to selling self-published books. See the resources section for suggested books to help you learn this process. (Quote Joe, author of Origin)

Get Connected

The online community loves sharing and talking. So meet other writers and connect with fellow bloggers. Bloggers are always looking for something to write about, many will be happy to give you a mention if you have something interesting to say.

If you are in a particular niche, you could get involved writing for magazines, local or national, to help get your name out there.

Be part of real and online communities, make connections and get the word out about you and your book.

Join in the conversation and get your name known out there and you'll be surprised what opportunities come your way.

Conclusion

You've dreamed about writing a cookbook.

Now you have all the information to empower you to get on and do it.   Are you going to take action to make your dream a reality?

Here's a thought-provoking quote from one successful entrepreneur:-

> *If you think you can do a thing*
> *or think you can't do a thing,*
> *you're right.*
>
> Henry Ford

So, what are you waiting for? There has probably never been a better time in history to get your book published.

With the availability of print-on-demand books and the rocket rise to success of ebooks, you can get your book out there, fast!

All the traditional challenges to publishing your book no longer apply. You no longer need to find a publisher and self-publishing is now incredibly cheap or free.

So, if you are still passionate about writing your cookbook, what is your next step?

Why not take the first steps right now?

- Start brainstorming and writing down your ideas
- Write down a date that you write your book by
- Tell someone you're going to write a book

You can start your journey to becoming a published author today – will you?

I really hope so – and look forward to seeing your name on the list of best-selling cookbook authors real soon!

All the best,

Jen

Appendix 1 - Finances & Costs

If you get it right, you can make 70% profit from your book rather than the meagre 15% or less that a publisher might offer you.

Kindle

All books priced between $2.99 and $9.99 (or equivalent in other currencies)may opt in to the 70% royalty option offered by Kindle. Books priced under $2.99 or over $9.99 earn a 35% royalty.

Do not forget to edit "Your Account" details to specify the bank account where any royalty payments should be sent. Royalties accrue separately for each Amazon marketplace . The balance of each account will be paid 60 days after the end of a month, as long as you have accrued a balance of at least $10/£10 for electronic funds transfer of $100/£100 for payments by check.

Createspace

The Royalty Calculator makes it quick and easy to work out how much money you will make per copy sold. By upgrading to the Pro Plan for your book, you will earn a higher royalty per copy for a small investment (Pro Plan upgrade, per title costs $39).

Should you upgrade to Pro Plan for your cookbook? Calculate the royalty you will earn with and without Pro Plan. Estimate how many sales you expect to make over the lifetime of the book and see how much royalty you would lose without Pro Plan.

Example

A book of 108 pages or less costs $3.66 to print (or $2.15 with Pro Plan)

For a book selling at $8.99, you will earn $3.24 on Pro Plan

A book selling on Amazon at $7.77 earns a royalty of $1.00 per sale, or $2.55 with Pro Plan (i.e. after deducting printing costs and 40% of book's list price for Createspace percentage).

For example, a 100 page black and white book priced at $8.99 costs $2.15 to print *with* Pro Plan or $3.66 *without*

Pro Plan. Add in a 40% profit share taken by Createspace is $3.60, leaves you either $3.24 royalty with Pro Plan or $1.73 royalty without. If you sell at least 26 copies, you will have recovered the cost of the Pro Plan for your title.

Example figures correct as at November 2011
Please check Amazon for the latest royalty figures and percentages

Appendix 2 - Resources

We include here resources that we have found useful along our own journey to publishing.

Writing A Book:-
Recipe Writers Handbook (Barbara Gibbs Ostmann & Jane Baker)
The Art of Creative Non-Fiction (Lee Gutkind)
Writing Successful Self-Help and How-To Books (Jean Marie Stine)
The Wealthy Author (Joe Gregory & Debbie Jenkins)

Self Publishing:-
Aiming at Amazon (Aaron Shepard)
Perfect Page (Aaron Shepard)
POD for Profit (Aaron Shepard)
The Self-Publishing Manual (Dan Poynter)

Promoting Your Book:-
ePublish (Stephen Weber)
Frugal Book Promoter (Carolyn Howard-Johnson)
Plug Your Book! (Steve Weber)
The Wealthy Author (Joe Gregory & Debbie Jenkins)

The Well-Fed Self-Publisher (Peter Bowerman)

CreativePenn blog by Joanna Penn - www.thecreative-penn.com

Cookbook Indexing:-

http://www.culinaryindexing.org/indexers.html - for a selection of culinary indexers

Norene Gilletz, www.gourmania.com

Please note, inclusion in the above list does not qualify as re-commendation.

Book Covers & Illustrations:-

www.fiverr.com - commission covers, illustrations and press releases for just $5

www.elance.com - put your project out to offers from a wide range of experienced designers, editors, etc, then select the one you wish to work with

Photographs & Stock Photos:-

www.sxc.hu - free, make sure to read the conditions of use

www.istockphoto.com - for a wide range of beautiful photos, starting at under $5

Copyright Law:-

http://www.writersservices.com/wps/s1_copyright_la
w.htm

http://Publishing-contracts.co.uk/ - SEQ legal offer
ebook agreements, legal and copyright notices

ISBN (International Standard Book Number):-

In the UK:- http://www.isbn.nielsenbook.co.uk/
Elsewhere:- http://www.isbn.org/

About The Author

Jen Carter is a best-selling Amazon author, selling a number of books under different pen names on Amazon.

You can find her daughter, Alissa Carter's cookbook, *"Healthy Breakfast Recipes"*

for sale at Amazon, Barnes & Noble and online bookstores.

Disclaimer & Terms of Use

(1) You must not in any circumstances:

(a)   publish, republish, sell, license, sub-license, rent, transfer, broadcast, distribute or redistribute the ebook or any part of the ebook;

(b)   edit, modify, adapt or alter the ebook or any part of the ebook;

(c)   use of the ebook or any part of the ebook in any way that is unlawful or in breach of any person's legal rights under any applicable law[, or in any way that is offensive, indecent, discriminatory or otherwise objectionable];

(d)   use of the ebook or any part of the ebook to compete with us, whether directly or indirectly; or

(e)   use the ebook or any part of the ebook for a commercial purpose.

You must retain, and must not delete, obscure or remove, all copyright notices and other proprietary notices in the ebook.

The rights granted to you by this notice are personal to you, and you must not permit any third party to exercise these rights.

If you breach any of the terms of this notice, then the licence set out above will be automatically terminated upon such breach (whether or not we notify you of termination).

Upon the termination of the licence, you will promptly and irrevocably delete from your computer systems and other electronic devices any copies of the ebook in your possession or control, and will permanently destroy any paper or other copies of the ebook in your possession or control.

(2)   No advice

The ebook contains information about writing & publishing. The information is not advice, and should not be treated as such.

You must not rely on the information in the ebook as an alternative to legal and/or financial advice from an appropriately qualified professional. If you have any specific questions about any legal and/or financial matter you should consult an appropriately qualified professional.

You should never delay seeking legal advice, disregard legal advice, or commence or discontinue any legal action because of information in the ebook.

(3)   Limited Warranties

Whilst we endeavour to ensure that the information in the ebook is correct, we do not warrant or represent its completeness or accuracy.

We do not warrant or represent that the use of the ebook will lead to any particular outcome or result. In particular, we do not warrant and represent that by using the ebook you will [specify result] [or [specify result]].

To the maximum extent permitted by applicable law and subject to the first paragraph of Section [5] below, we exclude all representations, warranties and conditions relating to this ebook and the use of this ebook.

(4) Limitations and exclusions of liability

Nothing in this notice will: (i) limit or exclude our or your liability for death or personal injury resulting from negligence; (ii) limit or exclude our or your liability for fraud or fraudulent misrepresentation; (iii) limit any of our or your liabilities in any way that is not permitted under applicable law; or (iv) exclude any of our or your liabilities that may not be excluded under applicable law.

The limitations and exclusions of liability set out in this Section and elsewhere in this notice: (i) are subject to the preceding paragraph; and (ii) govern all liabilities arising under the notice or in relation to the ebook, including liabilities arising in contract, in tort (including negligence) and for breach of statutory duty.

We will not be liable to you in respect of any losses arising out of any event or events beyond our reasonable control.

We will not be liable to you in respect of any business losses, including (without limitation) loss of or damage to profits, income, revenue, use, production, anticipated savings, business, contracts, commercial opportunities or goodwill.

We will not be liable to you in respect of any special, indirect or consequential loss or damage.

(5)   Digital rights management

You acknowledge that this ebook is protected by digital rights management technology, and that we may use this technology to enforce the terms of this notice.

(6)   Governing law

This notice shall be governed by and construed in accordance with English law.

Printed in Great Britain
by Amazon